Mending the Nets

Mending the Nets

Poems by

Maureen McDole

Cover design by Shay Culligan
Cover image *Ocean 15* by Oliver L. Jackson Jr.
of Blaquejack Studios
Author photo by Maureen McDole

ISBN: 979-8-90146-710-7
Library of Congress Control Number: 2026934950

Kelsay Books
502 South 1040 East, A-119
American Fork, Utah 84003
Kelsaybooks.com

For my mother, Kathleen.
Thank you for making me.

And for Florida.
Thank you for making me, me.

Acknowledgments

Thank you to the following publications, where versions of these poems previously appeared:

2023 in a Flash: Scars Publications 2023 flash fiction and art collection: "Jaws" (reprint)

The Artisan: "Wild Country"

Chameleon Chimera: An Anthology of Florida Poets: "My Grandmother's Curtains" (reprint)

Down in the Dirt: "Great Grandmother," "Jaws," "My Grandfather's Typewriter," "The Beach at Night," "The Pink Castle"

Moonstone Anthology: "My Grandmother's House"

Moonstone Pure Ink Anthology: "The Red Shag Carpeted Stairs" (reprint)

On Stones and Bones: Scars Publications 2023 poetry and art collection: "Great Grandmother" (reprint)

Quail Bell: "Mending the Nets," "The Red Shag Carpeted Stairs"

The RavensPerch Journal: "Our Lady of Sorrows," "My grandmother's Perfume," "Grandfather, the Fisherman," "Family"

South Florida Poetry Journal: "My Grandmother's Curtains"

Writing in a Woman's Voice: "Without Words"

Contents

Perhaps this is the most important thing for me to take back from beach-living: simply the memory that each cycle of the tide is valid; each cycle of the wave is valid; each cycle of a relationship is valid.

—Anne Morrow Lindbergh, *Gift from the Sea*

Mending the Nets

I was cast in the nets of a fisherman family
in hurricane force winds, poetry-filled
among wounded souls and the spiritually poor.

Dysfunction distilled in my barrel
from an early age.

Home was everywhere—there were droves
of us—but we had *nowhere,*
my territory boundless, suffocating
in its loneliness.

I was rudderless, surrounded by people
run aground after losing their North Star.

Our compasses haywire, our courses set
for destruction, drugs and alcohol
served in the tangled net of disruption.

Strife was the special of the day.

The tides ruled our lives, but no one tasted
the moon. We were caught in the nets we wove
together, alone, each longing to be free.

The elders' faces wrinkled
with confusion and uncertainty.

As an adult I found my current
and became the sea.

Family Secrets

Our family reeked of broken promises.
Truth slipped through the stench;
I cast nets to nowhere. I searched everywhere
for validation, my ear pressed against a conch shell,
the ocean sound reminding me
this isn't how life is supposed to feel. Books bloomed
possibilities in my palms, offered an escape,
showed me there was more than this current.
Our story was a stormy tragedy. We didn't have friends
outside the family. Only mingled with our own. *Don't share
the family secrets:* a phrase I often heard. No one asked
how I was doing. In sixth grade, I wrote a story about a girl
whose friend kills herself. I won the writing award,
but no one asked about my home life.
I was smart and got good grades,
so everything was fine, right?

Real Magic

Florida marrow grows in my bones. Both my parents grew from deep in the Florida earth, and all my grandparents arrived in this nest when they were very young. They tethered our lives to the water. My father was a sailor, and my mother's side made their life among fish. If I leave too long, I grow barnacles—a mermaid can never stay stagnant.

At the same time, my home on dry land is a wild place that humans try to tame, but somehow it always takes back what was stolen. We think of Florida as beaches and Disney World, with nothing in between, but the interior with its live oaks dripping Spanish moss, swamps and freshwater springs, is like reading a weathered novel. When you crack it open, the dust scatters in your eyes, making you see real magic.

People who love Florida *really* love Florida. It's like we're all in on a secret, and we laugh at those who make fun of our state. Don't get me wrong, we have our problems, lots of them, but those are all human-made. All you need to do is take a kayak ride down Silver Springs or sit on the white sandy beaches near my home in St. Petersburg, on the West Coast of Florida looking out at the Gulf of Mexico, to realize this place is pure magic.

Soundtrack

Sea crystals shine past jellyfish plasma;
foam whispers and seaweed dances, snaring
my attention, begging to embrace as I stingray
shuffle along the sandy foundation of the earth,
as the clouds drift towards the sun's watchful eye,
longing to be included, and the moon rises behind
burgeoning cumulus cushions—the soundtrack
of my youth.

Finding Ways to Thrive Along the Disturbed Edges of My Family

Growing up, the only time I truly felt solace was alone in my room with my music blaring. My favorite songs cradled me as tears rushed down my cheeks, and I'd daydream that there must be a place where I'd be seen and understood. Being in public was a sharp jab to my side. I was a burden on everyone, and I could tell by their plastic smiles and sudden departures, people merely tolerated my presence. That's what the heavy, weighed-down, tear-soaked, young-person-Me thought, anyway. There's still some residue of her in my adult life. I always fear that eventually people will get annoyed with me and show me the door. I'm shocked when people want me to stay longer than the time I allotted for our interactions, and when I am invited to things in the first place. These friends have taught me that I am someone who brings full albums of joy to all my interactions. And when that sad-soaked-Me surfaces now and then, I give her oodles of kind words and serious acts of love. Then I shut the door on allowing her to control my life anymore.

Swimming Through It All

Every other day I stretch on my swim cap and goggles and slide into cool water. I've done this for years. Some days it's sweet sailing down my lane, but other days, it takes sheer willpower to complete my mile. The first six weeks of this new lifestyle were the hardest, not only physically, but emotionally. Primal screams erupted underwater, and all the baggage buried in my bones streamed to the surface of my consciousness to be released. I was swimming through all my shit: letting it go with each lap. To say my swimming practice has been life-changing is a profound understatement. My job is to jump in and let the water rearrange me. The wake I've made swells into every area of my life, and the results are infinite. I exercise to celebrate my body, not to punish it. In the last couple laps of each swim, I tell my body, "I took care of you, now you take care of me." I am profoundly grateful.

Mystery Bag

My first job: catching pinfish for the overnight fisherman to take on my grandfather's 24-hour charter boat to Florida Middle Grounds, located 80 miles off the west coast of Florida, limestone reefs that are home to the big fish. He was the first person on the Gulf Coast of Florida to take a charter boat out there in 1954. My grandfather paid us ten cents a fish, and I'd sit out on the Hubbard's Marina dock in cut-offs and an oversized T-shirt and patiently catch fish until I earned enough money to run up on the boardwalk and grab a gift, the fish kept alive in a big bucket of salt water at the end of the dock. I picked a brown paper bag out of a big barrel in one of the gift shops. It was a mystery bag, and I never knew what waited inside other than assorted little toys and candies. $1 was written in black magic marker on the front of the bag, and it took ten fish to open this surprise. Throughout my life I have patiently waited to catch so many slippery opportunities, filling up my mystery bag with the hopes of hooking success.

Grandfather, the Fisherman

At home he always wore
red and white striped boxers.
Barefoot. Legs crossed,
blue sapphire ring on his left pinky.

Curly gray hairs sprang
off his chest—I had never seen
gray chest hairs before.
My father was never
vulnerable like that.

In public Grandfather always wore
khaki pants or shorts
and a khaki shirt crowned
with a captain's hat—a General by day.

Red and green socks
for port and starboard
hugged his feet
whenever he left his home.

I remember how slowly he ate cheese
and crackers. How he savored every bite.
His discipline, pleasure. Way of eating:
calm in the storm. His nose in a book
or the *St. Petersburg Times.*

After my grandfather passed
the men in my family honored him
by fishing and wearing socks

that matched his. I write books
and let pleasure guide words
from my heart. My page catches them
like slippery fish.

Mangroves

pop as we glide in our kayaks.
Mangrove fingers massage us as we pass.
Who else senses we are near?
What creatures live beyond the brush?
The water shimmers its camouflage,
dancing shadows across surfaces.
Tunneling through the mangrove womb,
the amniotic fluid of sea life surrounds us.
Our coastal guardians protect us,
even as we bulldoze them,
indifferent.

Alone

My skin used to scream at the thought of being alone. I thought I would suffocate. I would never be able to connect with another person and would always be the punk song no one understood the lyrics to. Now I crave my quiet time. Once I met myself, I really enjoyed my own company.

I often crack myself up, and I'm amused by my sense of humor and way of moving through the world. I'm actually astonished when someone doesn't like me, but secretly I'm still that young girl who doesn't expect to be invited anywhere.

I don't know if that ever goes away when you feel alone a lot as a child. There's always a fear that your secret will get out, and everyone will realize you are really not that interesting or are actually a big pain in the ass, and they'll ask you to leave. That might be another reason why I enjoy my own company.

I never will ask myself to leave.

Becoming Visible

To prove I was visible
surrounded by family
who treated me as invisible,
I wrote.

My family seemed to not want to know me,
and I carried this knot
into every relationship.
At any moment
someone who spent time with me
could discover I was unlovable.

My safe space:
pen to paper,
sliding my emotions
across the lines
of my notebook.
This is how
I survived my youth—

this paper trail
of my value:
evidence
that in some way,
I too existed.

Saltwater Escape

Everyone was on good behavior at the beach.
The pink castle in the background: our fiefdom.
The salt air calms everyone's hurt.
                Playfulness   was allowed.
                We could be children at the beach.
The oppressive air of my household
                                washed   out   to   sea.
The Gulf of Mexico spelled freedom.
I imagined
                                        a whole other life
on the other side of the horizon.
                The negative ions
cleaned out my sensitive soul. The waves held me.
The sun claimed my fair skin. Pain so acute
even the sheets were heavy hands
                                    on my pink skin.

The Pink Castle

I spent one summer living at my grandparents' house directly across the street from the Don Cesar Hotel on St. Petersburg Beach. Every night its pink castle glow lulled me to sleep. The pink glow must have entered my mind and made me a poet. Our parents worked and often left my cousins John, Micheal, and Colin at the house with us. It was the early 80s, and MTV was king of our castle. We'd flip a coin to see who would go into Grandma's room. We wanted $20 to fill ourselves on video games and ice cream across the street at the hotel. It was the scariest thing to enter her room and ask, but she would always creep up from bed and say, *Oh honey, of course. Grab my purse.* To this day, I hate asking for money. I always got mint chocolate chip or orange sherbet. We deposited our borrowed quarters in Pac-Man, Space Invaders, and Centipede until our pockets contained only crumbs. These moments were the freest I ever felt as a child, safe with my cousins in the pink castle. That summer I discovered HBO late at night and had my first introduction to sex on TV. I'd sneak downstairs after everyone fell asleep. I told myself I had insomnia from sleeping in a foreign house, the pink light. We never had cable at home or money for ice cream and video games. My grandparents' house was a portal into a richer, more sensual world.

The Red Shag Carpeted Stairs

that led to the upstairs bedrooms
in my grandparents' house
marked my safe space between
two worlds: the private parties
upstairs with whispers that hung ripe
in the air, and the laughter, booming chatter,
and flashes of anger that flooded
the spaces below.

All of us kids would gather
on those red shag stairs
during Christmas, Easter,
and family reunions.
I would run my fingers along
the red strands on my own step
and regroup.

I grew tall and realized
that I feel overwhelmed after
a few hours in the company
of *anyone,* so it's no wonder
that I often ended up in tears
whenever I spent too much
time away from those
red shag carpeted stairs.

I Remember

sitting in a room with thirty family members
and feeling alone. I was the dramatic one,
bawling in the bathroom, the air so sick
because of condensation in my tears.
I was the crazy one, the canary
at the cocktail or Christmas Party;
the air wasn't breathable.
I watched everyone choke
with grievances and grudges.
Every member of my family longed
to be reeled away, out of the sea. You see,
I emerged from the womb screaming
punk rock anthems of rebellion.
The status quo: not sustainable.
I was wired to thrive. They say we choose
our family. Hardships early on breed empathy.
More than anything I wanted to be saved,
a life raft guiding me back to friendly shores
that I saw existed in books.

Grandma Speaks

I bring Grandma fluffy scrambled eggs,
rye toast triangles, and freshly brewed coffee.
She is sitting up in bed
staring at her fluorescent fingernails.

She asks me what I've been doing
all morning. I tell her I've been writing,
because if I don't write everyday
I feel waterlogged. It's how I process
my powerful emotions.

She leans forward, says,
How did you know to do that,
to be so introspective?
I tell her how reading books
awoke the desire in me
to write.

She sips her coffee and says,
You must really know yourself.
I don't imagine I know myself at all,
and looks up to the ceiling.
Well, Grandma says, staring straight
into me, *I was never taught*
to think I should.

My Grandfather's Typewriter

My teenage bedroom was two miles from the family business at Madeira Beach. It wasn't big, so I emptied the closet except for a desk featuring my grandfather's typewriter. Same typewriter he used to compose his fishing reports for the *St. Petersburg Times.* On the wall I hung a map of the world above the bookcase with rows of *The New Book of Knowledge.* In my closet, I'd pretend I was a journalist, my dream when I grew up. I never imagined anyone would want to marry me, so I picked out a place on the map—the one imprinted on me by infomercials about the AIDS crisis—and saw myself living there: wandering Africa in a long braid, seeing places as a photographic journalist, maybe adopting a child. I never got to Africa, well not yet anyway, but I did grow up to be a writer and adopted my youngest sister's child. And I wonder if all those childhood images are still there, collecting dust in the drawers beneath my grandfather's typewriter.

Ars Poetica in Prose

The teenage me tried to talk everyone into being the best version of themselves they could be. I was surrounded by kids whose homes were broken, missing a parent, or didn't exist within houses. They were in survival mode, numbed themselves with alcohol and drugs. I tried to make them forget their needles, shoot up with sunshine instead. They only felt irritated, resented my sunshine shots because they couldn't think about anything more than surviving day to day. This wasn't failure, though: it was my early training as a writer. As I grew older, I realized I had to weigh my words carefully as my best way to help heal the world. Anyone who chooses to pick up a book that I wrote makes the choice to hear what I have to say. Ever since, my daily practice is to choose my words, but sometimes I slip up and just wanna spread the love. More often than not people are open to what I have to say, but sometimes my phrases fall on locked ears. Just focusing on writing is the best use of my energy. I feel more fulfilled and less frustrated if my words don't land right, sunny side up. As writers, we always wish our words safe landings.

Home Base

The Gulf of Mexico has always been my sanctuary. When I'm away, I come untethered—set to drift on seas of city and concrete, no way to flow. In my Pinellas County home, I nestle between the Gulf and Tampa Bay. If scientists were to someday study my DNA, they'd see images of a peninsula on a peninsula under their microscopes.

I tried to live in the mountains of North Carolina for eight years but never felt at home. Though I still visit regularly, the stagnancy starts to smother me, and after only two weeks I crave my watery home. Staring over the horizon from any of the five beaches I frequented as a child, the sunset assured me I always had an escape. I knew I could get away if I needed to—the irony is that this is where I always return.

When I became a mother, I couldn't imagine raising my child anywhere beachless. When I went to New Jersey, I couldn't believe you had to pay just to walk on the sand, and it's so strange not to see the sun set over the sea. In Florida we have beautiful white sand beaches that sparkle with magic in the moonlight. Watching the sun set over the water while the moon rises behind you in the east settles a primal feeling into your stomach. The sky flashes violent oranges and yellows; behind you, gorgeous purples and blues sift. No two sunsets are alike, and they've made me a witness to the beauty of this earth.

As the sun sets, I walk the beach where my great-grandparents, grandparents, mother, father, aunts, uncles, and cousins all used to saunter past. Even so, I know I'm not treading the same beaches they did: our beaches have been dredged and re-nourished so many times; reshuffled by afternoon thunderstorms and hurricanes. Yet, I can feel their footprints under my feet.

The Beach at Night

I go to the beach two hours before the sun sinks into the sea. I have fair Irish skin, so my entire childhood I was terrified of blistering, screaming sunburns. Before I figured out the time I breathe best at the beach, I would feel jealous of girls that could lounge in bikinis at any time and not worry about getting burned. My sister Alicia could handle the striking sun. She was a lot thinner than me, so no one made her feel she should cover up. All summer, she'd make her home at the beach. This was way before any of us thought of skin cancer.

When I was in my teens, I was the typical punk rock kid who wore black T-shirts and would never be caught in a bathing suit. Over the years, I've learned to embrace my body and breathe with ease in a swimsuit. This translated into my love of swimming laps at the pool and feeling comfortable showing longer stretches of skin.

My favorite time at the beach is night, but I never feel comfortable going there alone as a woman. It's frustrating that there are so many places women don't feel comfortable going alone because we have not created a society that is safe for us. Thankfully, the man I am with loves the beach at night as much as me, so every Monday, when most of the beach towels have already been hung in their homes, we start our week watching the sky streaked with the pink and yellow highlighters of my youth.

I Have Never

looked at my attractiveness as my currency;
I used my personality, wit, sarcasm to win people over—
I have never thought of myself as pretty.

I never caught the eyes of boys growing up,
and I still can't look into those windows of men
to catch their attention. I have never had a game

when it comes to dating, or realized how much
I used my personality until I was asked to model
on a daytime talk show. It was for Shapewear.

My friend, who was the host of the segment, loved
my curves, asked me to participate. As I stood in front
of the camera it hit me—

I have always used the fire of my brain and flavors
of my words to bring people into my world. Standing there
in front of those bright camera lights, curves and thick long hair,

being focused on this way was horrifying. And once
the segment was over, I rushed back into my house robe,
threw my hair in a bun, and devoured a thick, delicious book.

What I Learned From Books

I was hopelessly unprepared to live in the world. All my knowledge, the ways to be a citizen of life, rose from dusty book pages. I didn't know I should wash my face until at 30 years old I saw a friend rinse hers clean. I had never seen a healthy intimate relationship, only in the pages of a book. I am still a feral child. My parents were wounded, unprepared to grow into adulthood. I had to repair their mistakes, tidy my brain from the ground up. I am still a work in progress. But I am learning from living now. I see people who want to control the world at all times just to feel safe. The more secure I feel with myself the better I flow over bumps, blockades, and words. I spent so many years crying myself to sleep that I wake with gratitude every day I am alive. I see beauty everywhere now, even in people treading water through hard times, and I want them to get to the good stuff—to wade through this chapter to the one where they realize life is a good book.

Jaws

I refuse to let my child see the movie *Jaws*.
My life is divided into two scenes: before Jaws
and after. I used to swim in the Gulf without
thinking about how many fingers and toes
I could feel waving through the water, but now
every hair on my body is hyper aware—though
the chance of a shark attack is so rare, the fear
wells in me imagining Jaws' teeth splitting me
in two. I shriek if seaweed sweeps past my leg.
My friends who grew up in 1980s Florida feel
the same way: without the shark ever touching
teeth to our skin, Jaws scarred us. Now my child
is almost seventeen, and he swears to me
he still hasn't seen it.

My Restaurant Home

I was never a starving artist because I could always eat at my family's restaurant for free. When I was a kid, whenever I wanted to introduce a new friend to my world, I brought them to The Friendly Fisherman with not a dollar in our pockets. It was my family's restaurant in Madeira Beach and was built by my father in 1978, four years after my birth. My mother was the restaurant's general manager for three decades. The Friendly Fisherman was the closest thing to a steady home that I had. As soon as my friend and I sat down, we always ordered cheese squares and Timmy Nochman's fish spread as appetizers. I still dream about the steak fries. Stuffed fish from my uncles' fishing trips lined the walls above the panoramic windows which overlooked John's Pass, and if we timed it right, we could see my grandfather's fishing party boats come in from half-day or all-day fishing trips. One of my uncles was usually the captain. Families streamed off boats and poured into our restaurant with their plastic bags of mangrove snapper that we grilled to perfection for $4.95 with all the fixings. The building was one big room that was floor-to-ceiling wood, and all the waitresses, unless they were new, called me by name. I still bond with people over food, though now the food is prepared in other people's restaurants. Most of my friends now have never even eaten with me at The Friendly—that's what my family called it—since my mom retired over a decade ago. I always promise myself to go back with a new friend, but with the new management, I have to pay, and that takes away the feeling of home. To this day, if I'm out to eat at another restaurant, I have to remind myself that I have to close my tab. Because for a moment, I am back in a booth at The Friendly with a full plate of food and not a single guest check slipped my way.

Why I Hate Networking Events

I was always the girl with the red cheeks and sweaty palms whenever I had to find someone to eat my greasy spoon lunch with in the cafeteria, and my heartbeat sped up at recess when I was

expected to have a playmate, and again in science class when we were instructed to sit next to a partner. Now, when I enter *any* restaurant, the first thing I do is locate the chair against the wall

where I can get a view of everyone coming and going. I loathe being exposed. I need intimate one-on-one outings, and I only hang with people I know like the pages of my books. I joke that it

takes me five to 10 years to really get comfortable with somebody, but really it's the truth. I have always felt like a weirdo because other people seem to be able to navigate group situations at

schools or offices like a cool breeze, and they have no trouble plucking squares of cheese from trays at parties, bumping shoulders with the crowd and saying *Heyyyy.* We are all different

books, and we turn the pages in our own special ways. This is how we shake mountains. The status quo doesn't have to always be the default. We were never supposed to be made from the

same script.

Training Ground

My two older cousins on my mother's side, J and M, were so cool, a lot cooler than I was. As a teenager, I made it my mission to get them to like me. They read comic books, rocked out to the Dead Kennedys, wore long black trench coats and combat boots, and consumed *A Clockwork Orange* countless times. Deep in their own private conversation, they stuck together and talked shit at family parties, ignoring the mindless chatter and frequent arguments. I mastered the art of being a smart ass to win them over and to be included in their little group. I already knew how to use my intellect as a way to gain my father's favor, so this just added to my toolbox when communicating with men. The majority of the other men in the family were crass or disrespectful to women, so I fired my witty comebacks and strong feminist ideals, the perfect weapon to keep their inappropriate behaviors and comments on the ground. And even with all the early conditioning that clawed at all of us, I was never tricked into believing that I was the lesser sex. That time with family was a training ground and gave me even more fuel to bury my head into books. Because in my mind, brains always came before beauty.

Revolutionary Act

My new necessity: bringing rest into each jam-packed day of being alive. Rest, with her calm, pillowy presence, has become one of my best friends. Growing up, my bed was always my safe place where I could retreat after social school days. And when things were tense at home, I'd hide beneath my comforter. Sleep has always been a kind, deep friend to sweep away my obsessive thoughts and cradle me during my bouts of depression. Sleep smooths out my emotions like a cool breeze on a humid day. Lucid dreaming is my assistant for sorting out my problems. Every afternoon, rest waves me into bed. When we're young, we're handed nap rugs and quiet time. And now that I'm grown, I refuse to produce every moment of my day. I take note from the other animals and build sleep into my daily rhythms. Naps are a revolutionary act in our hustle culture.

Great Grandmother

Great grandmother Anna Hubbard was tired of life in her small Virginia town. At 17, she saw great grandfather Edward passing by on the train, so she jumped aboard and joined him in the carnival. Edward was a barker in the carnival, and Anna became a head and palm reader. My grandfather, Wilson, was born on the carnival circuit. When he grew up, he bought Anna a motel with his poker winnings as a way to keep his mother occupied and out of his marriage. Anna called her motel Hubbard House. It was on Eighth Street in Pass-A-Grille. But she still gave head and palm readings to her guests, and the sign out front flourished her skills.

I, too, was far from home when I was first introduced to tarot cards at college in North Carolina. A spark of fear told me that I was gonna go to hell if I touched those cards, but my grandmother's spirit was stronger than my Catholic upbringing. I've kept a deck of tarot cards ever since and use them daily. An important part of me is drawn to the esoteric arts, just as Anna was drawn to the train. I think our spirits must reach back farther than us because I have a blockage against wearing anything around my neck—I might have been hanged as a witch in a past life.

Like Anna's, my intuitive senses are strong, and I can read people and situations quickly. I've even matched up four marriages because I'm able to see connections between people who show they would make good partners. All the marriages are still together, and six children have been born of these unions. One marriage I've matched has lasted over twenty years. Sometimes, when I hold those cards in my palms, I can feel my great grandmother's hands.

Our Lady of Sorrows

My first dose of spirituality was Our Lady of Sorrows Catholic School, and as a word person, the impact that name had on me as a child pummeled my imagination. Statues of Virgin Mary

embraced me down every dusty hallway. I never really connected with God, The Father, but to have a woman lead my spiritual practice made me feel represented, seen, so I walked those

hallways with strong legs. I swung my arms, not afraid to take up space. And when I cried, I connected to Mary's sorrows. Decades later, Virgin Mary is still the prominent spiritual figure

in my life. The Divine Feminine is something that I've worked hard to express within myself, and that means loving all parts of me. I have this inner strength that knows I deserve to be cherished.

Those early images of the Virgin Mary imprinted on me that being a woman is powerful and divine, sorrows and all.

Forever

The brevity of life is becoming more and more acute with each day sailing past me. Maybe it's because I've breathed for nearly half a century, but I believe it's because with each passing day, I am more aware of the delicious wildness of life. I would need lifetimes to experience all the moments I wish for, and to read all the books that I crave, and write all the words that nestle themselves inside my mind.

Our days are tangled with the busyness of crossing items off lists, so we are starving for the juicy moments of actual living. This sends me frequently into a state of grief. And I love all of it—this thing called being a human—even when I'm in the midst of despair. I have learned to pluck lessons like fruit from the tree. I eat them, and I grow.

Words can never reveal all the feelings. Magic is sharing the feelings through holding someone's hand. It's the space where everything seems to stop, and all the worries and burdens just fall away, and I'm floating both through space and in communion with all that is. In these moments, I am hoping I can breathe forever as I soak up beauty after beauty.

Without Words

Even when I'm an insider,
I feel like an outsider—
like someone's gonna tap me
on the shoulder and whisper,
I know your secret.
You don't belong here.

You feel this way too,
don't you, dear human?

Look at us, alone
in our own thoughts,
searching for meaning.

I savor something in a book
or have an epiphany
about a random realization
and then try to articulate it
to somebody, but it's impossible
to translate the feeling,

and so the plump peach
of a moment becomes
a shriveled slice.

I wish that I could
hold hands with somebody
and transmute
what I'm trying to say
simply
through touch—

maybe that's why we crave
passionate intimacy—sex,
another form of communication.

How else can we transfer
the feeling
without words.

Dear Human,

When life shows up and reconfirms
its magic and generosity,
my tears run wild. Then laughter
arrives, then pure joy.
My deep heart's knowing
is confirmed, and I feel like a clear,
calm body of water able to reflect
the moonlight.

I think I came into this world
with the belief that we should all turn
toward the stars, but often we stay stuck
in our shadows.

When I read a confirmation
of all the possibilities of what it means
to be of breath and skin, I pause
because my tears bloom,
and my heart bows then bursts
wide open with thanksgiving.

These moments I wish to share
with you, dear human, but so much
of life is experienced
alone.

I wish that I could grab your hand,
transfer my feeling of joy to you.
But here is my attempt to put past feelings
into words that slide like sunlight
across the page, warming you.

Wildness

runs through every being of my family.
My family members become wizards
or land behind bars. A volcanic dissatisfaction
that often erupted into street brawls
and fist fights which always ended
with one of my aunts or uncles in jail.
Thank God for the family business
or many of them would have been unemployable.
My grandfather was always the one to bail
everyone out, but after he died, many members
further lost their way.

I packed my bags and headed
to the mountains. Sturdy, dependable,
they cradled my tattered edges.

A Basement in the Dark

When I was first out on my own, I fled to Asheville, North Carolina, inhabiting a series of basement apartments. For the first time, I felt I had arrived. I had a private space for $325 a month, safe and sustainable, something of my own. Yet with the series of basement apartments came a deepening lack of light. In escaping the darkness of my childhood, I left one cave to arrive at the mouth of another, and another. In the winter months, the only way to pass the time was to sleep. Squeezing my eyes shut was my only reprieve from loneliness. I passed through several of these dark apartments during my many breakups with the man who would become my husband, and the last time we split up was because of a basement apartment. In the bunker we shared, we slept underground, our mattress on the floor. The only light squeezed through a slit in the door leading upstairs to the yard above. I tried to rationalize that our love gave off its own passionate light when we were together, but the drab hopelessness of the space was enough to drive me back home to the Florida sun I craved. I arrived in August and didn't leave the beach. I tried dating other people because I knew I couldn't leave. My intuition told me. But G was the only man who seemed to understand the rest of me, who could offer deep intellectual conversation, and I tried to make that tenuous connection enough. *Fight Club* drove me back to him. After watching that movie, I realized he was the only person I could discuss it with. I found him settled into a house with a friend of ours. While I spent the next two years groveling and apologizing, he continued the profuse drinking he had begun in my absence. I would justify each glimpse of sobriety as a great new beginning for us, but his alcoholism always drove us back underground. We were living in a basement in the dark. We were briefly able to find the light together again, but it never lasted.

Shine a Light

I still have days when loneliness sticks to my bones. Maybe everybody does. Most people don't recognize my rhythm of occurring in the world. I can hear what they're thinking: *too much, too deep, overly sensitive.*

I hide myself and pop in and out with my friends. We all crave someone who will snap to our own unique beats. Here's what we need: someone to peer into all our dark corners, shine a light.

As I move closer to age 50, I realize the flashlight was always in our hands, and the only person that can brighten those dark spaces for yourself is you. And doesn't this make you want to break out in song?

But it is empowering, too, knowing that you can write your own tune. Don't get me wrong, I have darling companions in my life, some of the loveliest people in the world, but it's always lurking in the background—that existential loneliness that never quite leaves us alone. Listening to our internal music can make us feel truly at home.

Second Heart

The ending of my twenty-year
relationship took more than a decade
to overcome. Even after years of grief work,
I am still a well of deep wounds. Wounds
manifest in bodies and fester
if we let them. I thought we could feast
on our vows, forever.

We're surrounded by flashy ads to numb ourselves,
and it's no wonder that most people hand over the cash.
I hang my words like a lantern swaying in the storm
so they know they're not alone.

I went to see my cousin the herbalist
for symptoms of heartbreak.
He checked my tongue to detect deficiencies.
The tip screamed red, so he said,
No more heartbreak.

I write this now with absolute faith
that I will have a second husband someday.

I Still Dream About You

The dream goes like this. We are living in a big house chock-full of paintings, books, and pottery. It's always a different house in an exotic foreign location where there's a dinner party in full swing. Sometimes the waves sweep to our steps, and sometimes palm fronds brush our windows. The music is loud, and our friends hug hard. Last night I was in a black dress with red lipstick to match the flower in my hair. You and I were on a balcony under stringed lights. Inside, dessert was being served. But I always wake up in the dream and realize we're not together anymore. You always smile—you knew this moment was coming. I always remember and explain to you that we had five different types of love: Artists + Best friends + A shared history + Being parents. And marriage. We met in a high school art class. Perfect, since our life would be defined by art. When the marriage failed, we still had the other four loves to sustain us, but then your lying and addictions grew larger than us. (Of course I married an addict. I was built for it.) Once the best friend's love eroded, I knew I could find the other loves elsewhere and said goodbye. So why do we meet like this in dreams? Perhaps it's our souls deciding to mingle again, have a cocktail, admire some good brushstrokes—look at those colors. See how they once blended perfectly together, but do so no longer.

My Hours

I have always craved community. I've wanted to be seen, heard, appreciated, and not least, understood. I have wanted to feel like I have a home among people. I tried to create the home I wanted for my child, but outside of fleeting moments in the world, I only feel at home when I'm writing, reading, swimming laps in the pool, or dancing—in other words, when I'm making my own space. Sometimes I feel a profound sense of homecoming among my friends, the fizzing excitement of reunion, but often it is not until I leave that I can feel calm again. Perhaps this is why I was single for so long. Sometimes on a date I wonder, how do I do this? How does this work, again? I understand why some people choose not to get attached to anyone. I think I am like a pop-up store: open for a limited time, no standard business hours.

Growing Up Not Feeling Seen

Back then, I always had that one girl friend I walked through my days with. Usually she embodied the dominant personality, so I was free to daydream as she orchestrated the plans. Most of the time I went along with her requests. She tended to carry this description: dysfunctional home, had a pool, stocked pantry. One girl hurt me repeatedly, but I remained friends with her because she provided Oreo cookies, Stouffer's pizza, and MTV. I spent as much time with these friends as I could and worked to have an open ear to all their problems, hoping that they would eventually listen to mine, but their self-centeredness kept our narrative intact.

As I collected more years, I gradually moved on from these types of friends. Now I'm surrounded by lovely people who are as equally committed as me to being kind and ever-evolving. It's taken a decade to get used to this life. Sometimes I look at my friends, and I'm blown away that they *choose* to spend time with *me.* When you grow up not feeling seen, it's always surprising when people recognize the rhythm of your steps.

Public and Private Grandfather

When he was a teenager, my grandfather was the barker for the carnival's girlie shows. I still wonder how he felt about that, even when he visits me in dreams many years after his death. In the community, my grandfather loved to hold court and tell embellished stories to all who would listen; a formidable figure, no one dared question his word. But he had nothing to prove with me. He always asked how I was doing.

Grandfather wrote a regular fishing column for the *St. Petersburg Times* with the motto, *If you are too busy to go fishing, you are just too busy!* In public during working hours, he wore a full khaki uniform with his Captain's hat. For a night on the town, he always chose the most vibrant colors, enjoying the contrast to his monochromatic work uniform. At home, he was either reading in bed or at the kitchen table in his red and white boxer shorts, savoring the newspaper with a plate of cheese. With meals, his motto was, *Take small bites and savor your food.*

In public, a Crispy Cream cup filled with coffee and rum *for my bad knees* was a part of his uniform. The bottle labeled "Hub's Rum" sat behind the bar in the family restaurant within easy reach. Even well into his old age, the contrasts that formed the essential parts of him—like coffee and rum, barker and intellectual, monochrome and vibrant, wild stories and movie-star good looks—charmed everyone who crossed his path. I was no exception.

Growing List

My grandfather died when I was eighteen, and we tucked his favorite bottle of rum in the casket. He could continue to lace his morning coffee hereafter. No one else noticed Uncle Tommy in the kitchen drowning the bottle; he had snatched it from the casket. I just added the offense to my growing list of grievances: the uncles following me into quiet bedrooms where I went to escape the family chaos, always sitting too close, their beer breath leaning into me, trying to blow me over. Asking how big my breasts are now, if I am sleeping with anyone. The uncles: always the first to snap my bra when I pass, no one else in the family had my back.

Family

We hurt each other over and over—no one is safe, yet the word *family* keeps us sharing meals together.

We are soaked to the bone with brutality and bitterness—drenched pieces of paper—our stories blur—unable to live our own narratives—our ink muddled by sea air—we are tears and tight lips from family secrets with no resolution.

Disembodied dynamics—we are all loose-leaf paper—no binder to hold us together—scattering with the winds as a cold front roars in off the Gulf of Mexico.

We are boats banging into each other or chipping each other's paint—the barnacles of bruises crossed over—we are sharp to the touch—don't hug each other or you will get cut.

Eighteen

Punk rock music and club dancing offered me the freedom I craved. We were all outsiders together—the collective patched the loneliness.

I would change in the bathroom of Scotty's Hardware in Seminole where I worked as a cashier, then take off for a club in Tampa. I'd pop in Smashing Pumpkins or Tool in my Volvo station wagon's cassette player, head towards the Howard Frankland Bridge, and arrive before 10:30 pm so I could enter for free.

I went alone. I never drank. (It took me another decade to get drunk for the first time.) I danced until two in the morning and then drove back over the bridge towards St. Pete, but always after two bean burritos with sour cream from Taco Bell on N. Dale Mabry.

One night, there was a traffic jam on the bridge. The truck driver behind me came up to my window and asked what I thought happened. I said I didn't know, but asked him to flash his lights once traffic started moving so I could take a nap. He did, and after 30 minutes, I was back on my way. That's how trusting I was, how all of Tampa Bay was my home. I never felt safe in my family, but my sense of place was firmly rooted.

Dancing is still a trauma release. Today I dance to three songs every morning. Sometimes my bones crack, and tears stream down my cheeks because anxiety has drained from my muscles, and I've rocked myself back to life.

My Grandmother's Curtains

Pink sheer curtains swelled in the girls'
room when my mother was growing up.
She shared the pink shades with her sisters.
When I spent nights in that room, those curtains'
shadows scared me away from sleep.
A framed felt picture loomed over the hallway
that led to the bathroom: a group of dogs playing poker.
I swear they stared at me until I shut the door.
The walk-in closet was a meeting place for ghosts.
It wasn't safe to sleep with two eyes closed.
As an adult, I claimed the pink curtains
when my grandmother passed and the house sold.
I hung them in my bedroom and learned to love
the color they bred with the light. My once lover
named it *Womb Room,* a place I reclaimed.

Lorraine

Your face always rubbed off on me when I kissed you hello
because you never left the house without it on. I know
this is why I grew up having an aversion to makeup.
A man had to have *talent* to catch your eye, a twinkle,
otherwise what's the point?

That was the first question you always asked
about my dating life. Your moods had their own weather
patterns. You could have been an Indian Goddess
with your hissing wraith, mercurial in its destruction.

You were the greatest puppeteer I have ever known.
People danced around the strings you pulled. All of life
was a stage to you. Faye Dunaway would have played you
perfectly. You lived most of your life on Casablanca
Avenue in St. Pete Beach, your bedroom window engulfed
by the view of a pink castle.

I don't think there could be a more befitting backdrop
to your reign. A gunman opened fire
in a gay club in Orlando, murdering more than 50 people
this weekend. You would have been outraged.

Once you became a widow, priests and gay men
were your partners-in-crime. Your Catholicism and open-
mindedness were curious bedfellows, but I know you
expanded my worldview. You created a family of artists,
introduced us to beauty. Your life was an art form.
Red described you, even though you said a woman
should *never* wear it if she had any self-respect.

You're dying in our family cottage on Lake Michigan;
it's your favorite place on Earth. My mother
and aunt keep vigil at your side. The bed you are lying in
has rainbow sheets. I hope you feel like life delivered
your pot of gold. Your silver bangles remain my lucky

charms, jingling on my wrist as I write this to you.
I know a part of me formed from the recipe
that made you a woman. I am not sure what part,
but it has sweet and bitter ingredients.

I will spend a lifetime celebrating the good and releasing
the bad. I need to unpack your influence. Broken
and damaged souls ride in your wake, but your children
are devoted to you like no others; we forged a sacred oath
to defend your honor, rare in this day and age.

So Grandmother, you are the ideal, the matriarch
in a great American novel. Your life, a mythology.
We are all characters in *your* story. Once you pass on
we will be free to write our own, finally.

You weren't a maternal figure, you didn't take us
to Girl Scouts or on shopping adventures, you rarely
showed affection—we children were seen
and not heard—but your regal air and sophistication
laid my foundation, and I am proud to pass them on
to my child. I am honored to be named

Maureen Lorraine McDole. I know your resiliency
is the beams that hold up my inner strength.
I wish I could have hugged you enough
to have healed you.

Home

She is five years old, and her favorite spot is a bush under a live oak. The entrance is hidden to everyone but her. It's a refuge, the first place that feels like home. Every child needs to be held like this.

When she is fourteen and living in her family's eleventh house, she drags a mattress into the crawl space above the garage. She has to climb her dad's stack of ladders to access its plywood door: another refuge. High overhead, she reads books for satiating stretches. This is precious time that is not filled up by her younger siblings' or her parents' latest dramas.

In her twenties, in her first proper home, she is so proud of the brown leather couch she scored for free from a friend. It's okay that it dips a bit in the middle. Framed art posters decorate white walls. Kitchen dishes and silverware from Goodwill shine on the shelves. She knows she is rich because the hot water in the bath lasts until the tub is full.

Twenty years later, she has moved more times than she can count. For one four-year stretch she changed houses twice a year. Now she smiles seeing her housemate has replaced the window box weeds with shining sunflowers. She has started to feel settled in her bones.

The walls of her yellow two-story house hold pictures of black, brown, and white history, reflecting its occupants. The ninety-year-old hardwood floors have heard many stories. They love when the downstairs neighbor plays his trumpet. A blue jay family keeps her company when she sits on her front porch.

She is on a first-name basis with her mail lady. Everyone on her block adores her outside cat. She looks forward to the months when the frangipani and crepe myrtles bloom on her street. The southern magnolia tree outside her bedroom window explodes into white blossoms every April and May. She knows exactly where to park her car to get the most shade through the day.

It's easy in the quiet moments to forget those years in another house, when lights got shut off and she wasn't sure how she would pay rent. Doors slammed, then slowly reopened after fights moved through. Water boiled on the electric stove when the gas for the water heater was turned off so she could make a hot bath for her young child. This was the one time she tried to be married.

But that was long ago. She has made a better life for herself. *It's a foolproof system.* She repeats this to herself in moments of doubt. She loves her current home, feels whole there. She has only given the keys to those she loves and trusts.

The sun waves hello through her east-facing windows in the morning and goodbye from the west at night. She and her child feel that from now on, everything will be alright.

This is what makes a life, the brick and mortar of her days. Even when she moves from this house to experience a wider life, she knows she will carry this feeling with her. She knows it's within her and goes with her no matter where she lives.

Year after year she adds an extra coat of memories. The sidewalk covered in chalk art, the Christmas lights that stay up too long. The little moments that fit perfectly together into the word so much fuller than its four letters.

The Blue Hour

Liberation settles in
as we set off on our nightly walk.

You've been fixed in your classroom coffin all day
for ninth grade virtual school.

We shuffle into our second year of COVID-19.

It's fall everywhere we turn,
the ground littered with leaves
as live oak trees release them
to make room for new growth.

New beginnings dot the air.

Tomorrow, we turn the page to March—
one year since the world shut down.

Everywhere azalea bushes are in full bloom,
announcing themselves with light and deep pink
and white blossoms. The royal palms stand
at attention as we walk past.

We have only a fistful of years
before you leave this neighborhood
and our house for college.

I can't believe you are almost fifteen.

I am already grieving,
trying to prepare for the moment
everything changes between us
and you merge into the world.

I feel I have done a good job with you.

You are a kind, deeply
empathetic person, a hard worker,
seem to have a good grasp
on balancing work and play.

You know how important
it is to laugh often.

I pray you won't forget to eat
as you lose yourself
in your latest artwork,
and that you find someone
who loves you almost as much
as I do.

You are the love of my life.
I am an infinitely better person
for knowing you.

All this change feels too big
and too much,
but this is the journey
a parent must go through
to bless their child free.

The sun sets and the blue hour of twilight
falls upon us.

We round the corner towards our home,
and I instinctively grab your hand.

You let me hold it for the rest of the way.

Grandma's House

We are knee-deep in the remains
of my grandmother's house in St. Pete Beach,
her nest from 1958 until her death
one sweat-stained June.

These things I will miss:
psychedelic relics everywhere—
the neon flower stickers on closet doors,
faded rainbow prints in the stairwell.
The metal bread drawers in the cramped kitchen,
mold-green shag carpet in the dining room,
modern red chairs and couches
collecting dust on the oriental rug.
Creepy downstairs closet
that swallowed me in my nightmares.
Red shag stairs, the safe space
between parties upstairs
and heated conversations below.
The faucet in her bathroom
where I washed away torrents of tears
from my teenage and adult years,
and below my grandmother's sink,
the measure of my growth from girl to woman—
cold metal scale.

My Grandmother's Perfume

sat above the toilet in her black
and white tile bathroom with
its monogrammed hand towels.

Today, the bottle shines on my dresser.
I say good morning to Grandma
as I fetch clothes for the day.

Sometimes
I lift the orange flower lid
from the golden bottle,

Mariella Burani etched
in black across its front.
I hold it up to my nose,

smell the tang
mixed with baby powder,
and cry—

I have released
Grandma's spirit. She is here,
deep in the room with me.

I imagine her scenting herself
for a night out on the town
with my grandfather,

her dressing drink of Dewar's
and water helping her slide
into her party skin.

How to Describe My Childhood

If you've ever taken a writing class, you know what those teachers say: *Show, don't tell.* They say to do this with plenty of delicious, specific details. I keep thinking I need to be more concrete in my description of my childhood. Yet, so much of it was about the energy I was stuffed with: the claustrophobia, the loneliness. I felt hopeless, depressed, lost, unlovable, unappreciated, overly dramatic, and overly sensitive. Not seen. Not heard. Not loved. Sure, concrete things happened, but the overarching feeling was neglect, and there's not enough concrete in a lifetime to fill that void. I've had to rewire my whole life day by day, hour by hour, minute by minute. It's exhausting and all consuming, but then one day I started to feel a little lighter. In quiet moments, I watched as concrete drained from my bones. Each year I was freer than the last until I realized—I was always meant to build my own abstract world.

The Desk

1.

The only thing I wanted from her
was her wooden desk where she did all the bookkeeping
for my family's fishing boat and restaurant business.
She knew I was a writer and would always announce
that one day the desk would be mine.

It came with a wooden chair and a flower embroidered seat.
It came with the weight of Grandmother's hips.
It came with her brilliance and sweat smoothed into the wood
where she built a million-dollar empire.

Now I sit at that desk and build poems.
The topside of the desk has sliding doors.
I have lined them with postcards of Anaïs Nin, Langston Hughes,
and Georgia O'Keefe.

The desk came with a Georgia O'Keefe painting
and a matching rug. It came with her letter opener,
stationary, address labels, stamp holder,
and a box of coins. The desk came with her dreams
and exhaustion.

Sometimes, when I press my forearms
into the wood long enough, I'm not sure if it's me
or Grandma sliding my pen across these pages.

2.

I had to abandon the desk when I left
my apartment after nearly a decade.
We struggled for over an hour to maneuver
it through the door. Palms red, sweat dripping,
but its old screws were stripped, wood split
as we attempted to take apart its wooden bones.

I prayed to Grandma to help,
but she didn't respond.
For days I cried myself to sleep.
Now I have a new desk
in a new home, assembled
by my love. It waits patiently
for me to build my own empire,
Grandma winking from above.

Wild Country

I was not made to be subtle.
I must often break free.
I cannot be contained
in quiet domesticity.

My inner wild woman
finds her power within.
She will scratch the eyes out
of those who harm her kin.

Women are taught to be timid and meek,
to follow the rules and stay weak.
We can choose between being a Madonna
or a whore, but we are so much more.

Once we open the door to our freedom
and let the sunshine in,
the perfection polish wears off,
and with it comes a wily grin.

We see all the possibilities
of being fully ourselves.
We no longer put our desires away
or put our passions on the shelf.

I will never be satisfied being
quiet and demure.
I roar at conformity
and saying, *Yes, Sir.*

I am part poet/part wolf.
I follow the moon.
The dark doesn't scare me.
The night sky, my classroom.

I have learned to let my hair down
and let my spirit run free.
I was not made for confinement,
I am wild country.

About the Author

Maureen McDole was born in St. Petersburg, Florida. She is a direct descendant of carnies, carpenters, and fishermen. This do-it-yourself ethos in her DNA infuses every area of her life. As far back as she can remember she loved to write.

She is the author of three books of poems, *Exploring My Options* (2006), *Longing for the Deep End* (2011), and *Feast* (2021). She has an English BA with Literary Studies Concentration from University of South Florida and a Certificate in Arts & Culture Strategy from University of Pennsylvania. Her poetry has been set in a variety of different ways including: film, dance, spoken word, art installations, *Sprechstimme,* and traditional vocal works.

Maureen has been leading workshops and speaking about creativity and leadership for over 20 years. She founded the literary arts organization Keep St. Pete Lit in 2013 because she believes wholeheartedly in the power of literature to change the world.

She is the artist-in-residence at GISJane, working in the fields of water restoration, climate adaptation, nature-based solutions, and community resiliency. She lives in Minneapolis, Minnesota.

www.ingramcontent.com/pod-product-compliance
Lightning Source LLC
LaVergne TN
LVHW090536110826
845146LV00003B/1124

* 9 7 9 8 9 0 1 4 6 7 1 0 7 *